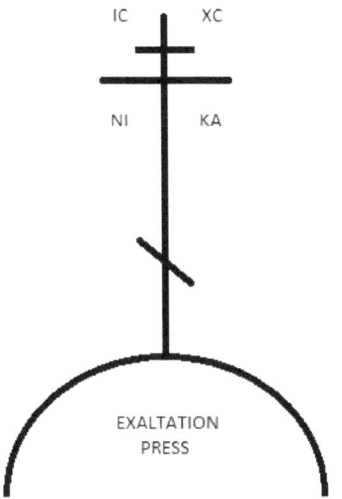

Approved for distribution by the Publishing Committee of the Russian Orthodox Church

From the series "Scripture and Feasts for Children"

Elena Trostnikova

The Nativity of Christ

Illustrations by Olga Podivilova

Translated by Fr. John Hogg

Grand Rapids - Exaltation Press - 2018

Copyright © 2019 Exaltation Press

Author: Elena Trostnikova
Illustrator: Olga Podivilova
Translator: Fr. John Hogg

"The Nativity of Christ"
 This book is part of the series "Scripture and Feasts for Children." It is about the Great Feast of the Nativity of Christ and is intended for reading to small children. The story here contained is structured close to the Gospel narrative, written in a simple and clear style for children with the addition of bright illustrations to help children understand as much as possible about the Savior's birth.
 The book also explains some of the traditional ways of celebrating Christmas and includes some simple Christmas carols for children to learn. The last section of the book "How to Read to Children About the Nativity of Christ," is a guide for parents.

All rights reserved. This book or any portion thereof may not be reproduced or used in any manner whatsoever without the express written permission of the publisher except for the use of brief quotations in a book review.

Translated from the original "Рожество Христово" by Nikea Press, Copyright © Trading house «NIKEA», www.Nikeabooks.ru

ISBN: 978-1-950067-02-2 (Paperback)

Edited by Cynthia Hogg

First printing edition 2018

Exaltation Press
Grand Rapids, MI

www.ExaltationPress.com

For bulk orders, please contact editor@exaltationpress.com

TABLE OF CONTENTS

Introduction - 10

How God Decided to Be Born on Earth - 13

The Announcement of the Savior's Birth - 14

How the Savior Was Born - 16

Who First Learned of the Savior's Birth - 19

The Wise Men (the Magi) and King Herod - 22

How the Magi Found the Christ Child - 25

What Herod Did When the Magi Failed to Return - 27

Return to the Holy Land - 30

How We Celebrate Nativity - 31

The Nativity Scene - 39

How to Read to Children About the Nativity of Christ - 42

Glossary - 51

INTRODUCTION - THE NATIVITY OF CHRIST

The birth of the Christ Child is one of the Church feasts that is most "child-like," in that it brings much joy to children in particular.

At the heart of this feast, the feast of the Nativity of Christ, is the fact that God came to mankind and became a human being. But how can we explain that to very small children – why it is that this day brings us joy, what exactly happened, and Who it was that was born? How can we convey to them what we, as parents and teachers, do not always have a firm understanding of and, even if we do, are often unable to explain it clearly?

For children two years and older, this book and its illustrations will help to tell the story of the Nativity. It is designed to be read lovingly by an adult, especially a parent, since at this age parents are a child's first teachers. The smaller children are, however, the more they love repetition and so moms and dads, grandparents, relatives, and friends will all find enough in this book to read and look at together.

The last section of this book is for adults and parents might find it beneficial to read through it in advance.

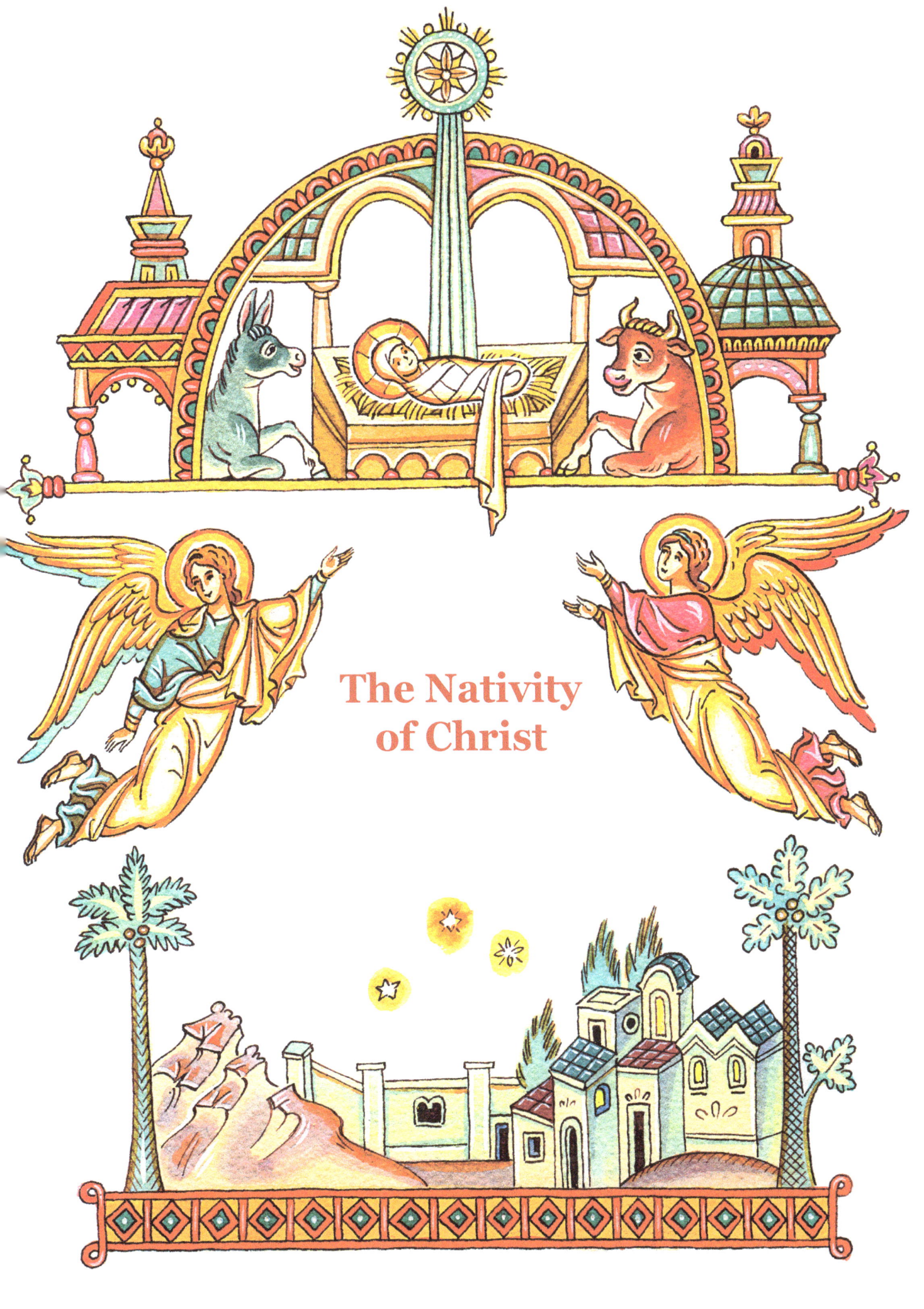

HOW GOD DECIDED TO BE BORN ON EARTH

God is the one who created and fashioned everything in the universe. Before there was anything, God existed. Our earth, the sun, the sky, the beasts and birds, the plants, the mountains and rivers – all of that He created with love. He loves all people. He loves you and me more than we know how to love. There is no end to His love.

And He created us, human beings, to be like Him and wants us also to love everyone.

But we stopped listening to God and forgot how to love and began to hurt each other. A lot of evil entered the world because of our sin.

And so, in order to teach us to love and be obedient, God decided to become one of us, to be born on earth among people, to teach us righteousness and goodness, and to save us from evil.

And in order to be born, He chose a mother for Himself.

THE ANNOUNCEMENT OF THE SAVIOR'S BIRTH

There is a place we call the Holy Land. The people in that land had not forgotten about God and were still waiting for Him to send them a Savior who would deliver them from evil.

In that country, in the small city of Nazareth, there lived a young woman who was kind and good, the Virgin Mary. She lived in the house of her elderly relative, Joseph, who took care of her.

The Virgin Mary became the mother of God when He came to His people.

This is how it happened.

When Mary was home by herself, an Angel came to her and said:

"Rejoice, O full of grace, the Lord is with you! Blessed are you among women!"

She was surprised and thought to herself, "What can this mean?"

The Angel said:

"Do not be afraid, Mary. God has chosen you. You will give birth to a Son, the greatest and most marvelous ever to be born. He will be the King of Heaven, the Son of God. You will give Him the name Jesus, which means Savior."

"How shall this be," Mary asked the Angel, "since I do not know a man?"

"For God, all things are possible. He will send the Holy

Spirit upon you."

"I will obey God's will," Mary said. "May it be to me according to your word."

The Angel left her and the Virgin Mary began to wait for the miraculous birth of God's Son.

HOW THE SAVIOR WAS BORN

Just like all children, the Son of God grew and developed in the womb of His mother, the Virgin Mary. Soon, the time was coming for Him to be born.

And just then, throughout the whole of the Roman Empire, an order went out to count how many people were living in each place and so all were told to go to whatever city their parents were born in and be registered there.

Joseph sat the Virgin Mary on a donkey and together they set out for the city of his family, Bethlehem. The journey lasted several days. And when they finally got to Bethlehem, it turned out that there was no place for them to stay. Many people had

arrived before them to be registered and so no one had any room for them, in their houses or in the inns. No one let them in. Night came and there was nowhere for them to hide from the rain and the cold.

In that country, there are many caves. Often, people even built their houses in caves since it was simpler – the house already had a roof and walls! And so Joseph found a cave where shepherds and their flocks would sometimes hide from the rain and the wind. Inside the cave, there was a manger – a long feeding trough where the shepherds put straw or other food for their livestock[1]. Joseph and Mary decided to spend the night there in the cave. And during the night, the time came for the Virgin Mary to give birth.

1 Words written in red are explained in the glossary at the end of the book.

And so the Son of God, the One that the Angel had told the Virgin Mary about, was born. He was a tiny little baby and His mother wrapped Him in swaddling clothes and laid Him in a manger for His bed, on the soft straw.

That little child was God Himself, who is the Savior of all people but no one on Earth knew yet that He had come into the world, that He had arrived and was born, not in a palace, but in a cave. No one except the Virgin Mary and Joseph had seen Him yet.

WHO FIRST LEARNED OF THE SAVIOR'S BIRTH

That holy night, not far from the cave, there were shepherds in the fields, watching their flocks by night. Suddenly, they saw an Angel, surrounded by a bright light. They were afraid but the Angel said to them:

"Do not be afraid! I bring you good news of great joy for all people! Today in Bethlehem has been born the Savior, the Son of God. He is Christ, the King of all. Go and you will find the

child in swaddling clothes, lying in a manger."

When he had said this, suddenly the sky was filled with a multitude of Angels, who praised God and said:

"Glory to God in the highest and on earth peace, goodwill among men."

When the Angels left them to return to Heaven, the shepherds said to each other:

"Come, let us go quickly to Bethlehem to see what has happened there that the Angel told us about!"

The shepherds hurried and soon arrived at the cave. There, they found the Virgin Mary, Joseph, and the Child lying in the manger. They worshiped Him and told Mary and Joseph about the Angel that appeared to them and how he told them that a Savior had been born and that they would find the infant Christ in a cave, in a manger for cattle.

"And then," the shepherds told them, "many angels appeared and the sky was filled with light! The angels sang, 'Glory to God in the highest and on earth peace, goodwill among men.'"

The Virgin Mary and righteous Joseph were amazed at what the shepherds told them. The Virgin Mary remembered every word and many years later, she told others about what happened as if it were only yesterday.

And the shepherds returned to their flocks, rejoicing and praising God for everything that they had seen and heard.

THE WISE MEN (THE MAGI) AND KING HEROD

In those days, in the holy city of Jerusalem, there was a king named Herod. He was wicked and clever and more than anything, feared that someone would take his kingdom from him.

And lo, from the far East, three Wise Men came to the holy city of Jerusalem. They were dressed in fine clothing that was not at all like what the people of Jerusalem wore. They asked everyone that they met on the way:

"Where is the newborn King? We saw His star in the East

and have come to worship Him."

Nobody could understand what they were asking about. And so, of course, they told King Herod about these strange people. He called together his advisers and the most learned people of his kingdom and asked them:

"What do your books tell you? Have you heard that some special King is supposed to be born? And if He is born, where is that supposed to happen?"

"Yes," his learned men answered, "our books that were written by the ancient prophets say that in Bethlehem a King will be born who will save His people."

Then Herod commanded them to bring the strange men from the East to him.

"Who are you?" he asked.

"We are Wise Men who study the stars and the earth. You call people like us Magi. We saw in the East a new star that showed us that the King, the Savior of His people, has finally been born! We have followed the star for a long time and finally it brought us to this Holy Land. We want to find the holy Child and worship Him."

Oh, how scared and furious Herod was! He did not want anyone else to be King. But he did not let the Magi see how unhappy he was at the news of this King's birth. Instead, he said to the Magi:

"Hurry! Hurry and go where the star leads you. Find the newborn King. And when you find Him, return to me and tell me where He is since I, too, want to worship Him!"

HOW THE MAGI FOUND THE CHRIST CHILD

And so the Magi went on their way to search for the Christ Child. The star showed them the way, moving across the sky until it rested over the house where the Child was. The star began to shine so brightly that the Magi understood immediately...they had finally found Him! They rejoiced greatly.

They went in and saw the wonderful Child, His mother the Virgin Mary, and righteous Joseph. They bowed down low before the Christ Child and took out their precious gifts for Him – gold, frankincense, and myrrh. Frankincense and myrrh are precious, sweet-smelling spices from the resin of rare trees.

These kinds of precious incense could cost more than gold. They were truly gifts fit for a King.

At night, when they were sleeping, they each had the same dream. An Angel told them not to go back to Herod but to return to their own country by a different way. And so they did.

When they left for their own country, an Angel appeared to Joseph in a dream and said:

"Go, take the Child and His mother and flee to Egypt and stay there until I tell you to return. Herod wants to seek the Child to destroy Him."

And while it was still night, before the sun rose, Joseph and Mary the Mother of God took the Child and set out on the difficult journey into the far country of Egypt.

WHAT HEROD DID WHEN THE MAGI FAILED TO RETURN

How angry Herod was when he realized that the Magi were not coming back to tell him where the future King was born! He almost burst with rage.

In order to destroy the Christ Child, he came up with a terrible, wicked plan. He remembered that his advisers had told him that the Savior King was supposed to be born in the city of Bethlehem. And so he commanded his soldiers to go to Bethlehem and kill all the young boys they found there so that the

Christ Child would not be left alive.

    Not all the soldiers agreed to obey such a wicked command. Some of them ran away from Herod so they would not have to kill innocent children. But some of them were willing and so they set off to carry out his terrible order.

    Those soldiers hurried to Bethlehem and began to kill all the young boys they found, like Herod had commanded them. Their mothers wept and tried to hide their children but were unable to.

God had pity on the children and when they died, He took all of them right into Paradise, the same Paradise where the first people once lived, where there is only joy and no evil. Time passed and they were reunited with their mothers, fathers, and new brothers and sisters in His Kingdom.

But the wicked King Herod soon died. Neither doctors, nor medicine, nor all of his riches, were able to save him from death.

RETURN TO THE HOLY LAND

When Herod died, the Angel again appeared to Joseph and said that they could return to their native city. And so Joseph and the Mother of God took the Christ Child, who had now grown a little, and returned to the city of Nazareth and began to live there. Jesus Christ grew and helped St. Joseph in his work. He learned and made His parents glad.

When He was grown up, He began to teach people about goodness and righteousness.

That is how God became Man. From then on, people, including you and me, know that God is with us, that He loves us, and that we should also be like Him. We should love all people like He does and do only what is good.

Every year, we remember the birth of Christ and celebrate it and rejoice. In honor of Christ's Nativity, people began to decorate Christmas trees, to give each other presents like the Magi gave Christ and, of course, celebrate Nativity solemnly in Church.

The twelve days after Nativity are called "the Twelve Days of Christmas." During this time, we glorify Christ by singing Christmas carols. In some countries, children gather together with one of them holding a star on a stick – that is very important! – and they go from house to house to greet all of their neighbors. In a small town, they might go from door to door while in a city, their friends and relatives might invite them over to their house. When the owners of the house open the door for the children, the children might say something like, "Let us, friends, glorify Christ" or "We have come to give glory to Christ and to bring you good cheer!"

Then, the older children who know the prayer called "the Troparion for the Nativity of Christ," sing it:

Thy Nativity, O Christ our God,
Has given rise to the light of knowledge in the world
For thereby those who worshiped the stars
Did learn from the stars to worship Thee, the Sun of Justice,
And to know that from the East of the Highest Thou didst come,
O Lord, glory to Thee!

This prayer tells us that Christ's Nativity brought to all people the light of knowledge and righteousness from Christ, who shines like the sun, the Sun of Justice. In it, we also sing about the Magi who studied the stars but who were taught by a miraculous star about the newborn Christ and to worship Him, the Sun of Justice.

Smaller children can also learn poems or songs about Christ's Nativity.

And the people who live in the houses give the children candies or other tasty treats.

There are many good Christmas carols in English that are suitable for Orthodox Christians to sing. A few of them are given on the next few pages.

O Come, All Ye Faithful

O come, all ye faithful,
Joyful and triumphant,
O come ye, O come ye to Bethlehem.
Come and behold Him,
Born the King of Angels!

O come, let us adore Him,
O come, let us adore Him,
O come, let us adore Him,
Christ the Lord.

Sing, alleluia,
All ye choirs of angels;
O sing, all ye blissful ones of heav'n above.
Glory to God
In the highest glory!

O come, let us adore Him,
O come, let us adore Him,
O come, let us adore Him,
Christ the Lord.

Yea, Lord, we greet Thee,
Born this happy morning;
Jesus, to Thee be all glory giv'n;
Word of the Father,
Now in the flesh appearing,

O come, let us adore Him,
O come, let us adore Him,
O come, let us adore Him,
Christ the Lord.

Joy to the World

Joy to the world! The Lord is come
Let earth receive her King
Let ev'ry heart prepare him room
And heaven and nature sing
And heaven and nature sing
And heaven and heaven and nature sing

Joy to the world! the Savior reigns
Let men their songs employ
While fields and floods, rocks, hills and plains
Repeat the sounding joy
Repeat the sounding joy
Repeat, repeat the sounding joy

No more let sins and sorrows grow,
Nor thorns infest the ground;
He comes to make His blessings flow
Far as the curse is found,
Far as the curse is found,
Far as, far as, the curse is found.

He rules the world with truth and grace
And makes the nations prove
The glories of His righteousness
And wonders of His love
And wonders of His love
And wonders, and wonders of His love

Then all together, everyone may play joyful winter games before going back home. At home, there is always the Christmas tree. In the cold of winter, other trees have lost their leaves a long time ago, but Christmas trees are still alive with green. Christmas trees should be decorated by Nativity. Traditionally, a star – the Christmas star – is put on the very top of the tree, sometimes with an Angel. All sorts of beautiful ornaments can be hung on the tree, to greet the Christ Child. Candies, nuts, and other treats may also be hung on the tree.

THE NATIVITY SCENE

Do you remember the cave in which the Virgin Mary gave birth to the Christ Child? At Christmas time, there is a beautiful old tradition of putting together Nativity Scenes, to represent that cave where Christ was born. Sometimes, you see them inside Churches, sometimes outside the Church, and sometimes at people's houses, under the Christmas tree or somewhere near by where it is easy to see.

The cave can be be made out of paper, a box, modeling clay, or even out of snow and ice, if it is outside. In the center

of the Nativity scene, there can either be an icon of the Nativity or a little figurine of the Virgin Mary watching over the manger where the Christ Child is lying. Surrounding them on all sides are those who were present at Christ's Nativity: Joseph, the donkey and cow, the shepherds with their sheep, the Magi with their gifts.

But there is also another way of putting together a Nativity Scene – as a live puppet theater where the children put on a play about the Nativity of Christ and about wicked King Herod. The Angels, shepherds, and Magi all make an appearance. The picture above depicts what this might look like. The theater has two levels. On the top level, there is the Christ Child in the

manger, the Virgin Mary, and Joseph. The Angel appears to the shepherds who come to worship the infant Christ, followed by the Magi. The lower level contains the royal palace with Herod sitting on his throne. At the end of the play, death comes for King Herod.

The other picture shows how older children might put on a play for younger children. They are dressed as the Angel, a shepherd with sheep, and one of the Magi with gifts for the Christ Child. They all find the way to the manger where the newborn Christ is lying. And the wise Magi asks the younger children riddles or shows them tricks.

HOW TO READ TO CHILDREN ABOUT THE NATIVITY OF CHRIST

Many parents have a hard time explaining the feast of Christ's Nativity to children who are still very little. This book is designed to be read to toddlers, even those who have not yet turned three, especially if they already enjoy looking at pictures and listening to their parents read to them. This is a good opportunity to teach our children the basics about God and the faith.

This book faithfully retells the story of the Savior's birth according to the Gospel narrative while structuring it in a way that helps a child understand as much as possible. Even a small child can understand the events as they are described by the holy evangelists Luke and Matthew. It is very important, however, that we do not tell this story to our children as if it were just another fairy tale. The story of our Savior's birth is one that they will hear over and over again in the course of their lives, and that will help to enlighten them.

Later in this chapter, you will find some notes and explanations for each of the earlier chapters that may help you answer your child's questions.

The first time you read this book with your child should be a joyful time for both of you, just like later on when you read it more slowly and attentively.

Begin with the front cover. Have your child name each person while pointing to them with their finger. It is very important that we choose the right names and words, so that they can connect with the illustration: "Look! Here is the Christ Child and that is His mother, the Virgin Mary."

When you open this book, you will notice the pictures that come between the covers and the pages of the book. These pictures depict a big, cheerful world. Take the time to look at all the pictures with your child, and ask, "Who is this? What is that?" pointing out the donkey, the little boys and girls, the Christmas tree, the Angel. "Look! Do you see the children carrying the star and singing?"

For children who are still very little, the whole book will be told looking at the pictures, probably many times. It is important that we also enjoy that process. Ask yourself if you understand everything or not. But remember that what confuses adults is often different from what confuses a child. Children can be surprised or puzzled by things that seem simple and understandable to us.

It is best not to read the whole narrative to a child at once but to read at most two or three chapters at a time. St. John Chrysostom recommended reading Bible stories to children at that pace, even to those children who are moving out of the toddler stage. Try to integrate all the pieces and pause for your child to digest and think about what you have read, and allow time for questions.

And so, read the book a little at a time, stretching it out over several days. Afterwards, when they have fallen in love with it, re-read it to them several times so that they can then start to look through it themselves, even if they have not learned to read, since they will remember the content.

Who is God? The Names of God and the Mother of God

In the beginning of the book, God is described in simple words that young children can understand without further explanation. The only thing that might be new to them is that when we talk about the newborn Child, from the very beginning we talk about Him as God who has come to His people. Later on, we introduce the concept of Him as "the Son of God." It goes without saying that the concept that God is Triune – the Father, Son, and Holy Spirit, one in Three Persons – is difficult for young children to understand. It is important, however, that they understand Christ as God, and not just God, but as God who became Man. A three-year-old or any preschooler should not be too confused about God simultaneously being the Son of God since this book treats it all very naturally.

The Savior calls Himself the Son of God and even more often, the Son of Man. The Archangel Gabriel calls Him the King of Heaven. His human name is Jesus, which the book explains means Savior.

The Angel, proclaiming the good news to the shepherds, lists several of God's names. "Today in Bethlehem, a Savior has been born, the Son of God. He is the Christ, the King of the world." Here we see that name, "Christ," for the first time. A more accurate translation of the name Christ would be "the Anointed One," since He receives by anointing the gift of the Holy Spirit, although at the time that the Savior was born, they were expecting Him to be a King. The Magi come to bow down before Him as a newborn King. And when His earthly life comes to an end, the inscription on the Cross reads, "Jesus Christ, the King of the Jews."

Is this too many names for a child to take in? Of course not! Children will hear all of these names for God from time to time. It is a good thing if, from the very beginning, these names are imprinted in their minds along with the Gospel story of His birth and the image of the Savior Himself.

The Virgin Mary first appears in this book under that name. Help your child see that she is not just a girl, but the first among girls, the most special of all. Later on, the book will call her "the Mother of God" which shows that she is not just any mother, but the Mother of God Himself.

The Announcement of the Savior's Birth – The Annunciation

The story of Christ's Nativity cannot be separated from the true beginning of the Incarnation, the Annunciation, which in Greek is called the "Evangelismos."

This word, which means "good news," or "the Gospel" is also the word that we use for the books about the Savior's life, as well as for the "good news" that the Angel gave to the Virgin Mary.

Luke the Evangelist recounts the appearance of the Archangel Gabriel to the Virgin Mary in the first chapter of his Gospel. Of course, parents should read that chapter in its entirety and reflect upon it.

In the book, certain phrases have been preserved that might be difficult for a child to understand. For example, in the description of the Annunciation, the Archangel says: "Rejoice, O full of grace, the Lord is with you! Blessed are you among women!" The Virgin Mary herself was confused by his words and reasoned within herself about what kind of greeting that might be (or as the book says, "She was surprised and thought to herself, 'What can this mean?'") Likewise, both children and adults, when they come across words in prayers that are incomprehensible, should imprint them in their memory, so that the meaning might be revealed later.

Children can learn the Archangel's words from the hymn, "Rejoice, O Virgin Theotokos…"

On the feast of the Annunciation (March 25th), it is wonderful to come back to this narrative with your child.

How the Savior was Born

The story of the birth of the Divine Child is laid out simply, faithful to the text of the Gospel of Luke, and without imaginative additions. More than likely, there will only be a few isolated words or concepts in this chapter that your child might not understand.

The first paragraph says that " the Son of God grew and developed in the womb of His mother." Fortunately, in the modern world, a large majority of children already know that babies grow in their mother's tummies. But if your family is an exception and your children still do not know where babies come from, you can use this book as an example to explain to them that babies are born from their mothers and that when a baby first appears inside its mother, it is very tiny but then grows inside her for a long time until the time comes for it to be born.

The Wise Men (the Magi) and King Herod

The story of King Herod and the Magi fits beautifully within the style of fairy tales that children are used to and so it is no wonder that it is often an integral part of Nativity plays. As a result, your child will likely absorb this narrative easily.

In ancient iconography, there are always three Magi and they are depicted as kings. You can tell your child that, according to an old Church tradition, their names are Gaspar, Balthasar, and Melchior.

What Herod Did When the Magi Failed to Return

The slaughter of the Holy Innocents is a very tragic story that would be difficult for children to take in if it were not for two factors. First of all, children are used to hearing fairy tales and in fairy tales, all sorts of bad things happen. But that would not be enough for a sensitive child if it were not for the second, much more important, factor. Christ is the victor over death. As Christians, we know that after their death, the Holy Innocents of Bethlehem truly went to Paradise and are counted among the saints, not just for pretend or as a kind of comforting fairy tale. In the book, this fact is both talked about and depicted clearly in the picture and seeing something with our eyes makes it easier to accept. If your child is tenderhearted and still feels horrified by the slaughter of the children, help them to overcome that terror with the help of the pictures. You can also look for depictions of Paradise in the pictures inside the front and back covers.

But no child will feel sorry for the evil King Herod who died an eternal death because his evil was justly punished.

How We Celebrate Nativity

This section deals in a simple and compact way with some of the old traditions surrounding how we celebrate the Nativity of Christ. It includes a few Christmas carols that have been chosen because they should be easy for children to learn so they can sing them at a family celebration or a larger Christmas gathering – at Sunday school, kindergarten, or at a get-together for a few families and their children.

It is always nice to put together a production of the Nativity story with dolls for the children in your family, perhaps using the ideas from this book. If your children are very little, the play can be very simple. Even a small production, put together with parental help, can make a large impression on a young child. If there are older children in your family, they can use their creativity and energy to take part in the preparations of the play, such as by making the dolls, and then they can put on their own performance. With small children, it is best to simplify things as much as possible, sticking to the story of the shepherds coming to worship the Christ Child and the Magi following the star to find Him, leaving out the part with King Herod. Even without that, the production will have an emotional impact on them.

It is another matter if you are putting together a Nativity Play with your friends and relatives. There is nothing quite like theater in the home! Hopefully, these kinds of Nativity Plays will become more and more frequent so that children will have more of an opportunity to see and participate in them.

If a group of older children, ages six to twelve, is getting together, you can suggest to them that they take on the roles of particular Magi and shepherds and act out scenes, adding additional elements to the festivities, like processing around the Christmas tree or coming up with riddles (after all, the Magi are wise men!) or other things that they can come up with through imagination.

Each family will need to form these Christmas traditions from scratch but what a joyful task that is, full of God's grace!

At Nativity, we also greet our friends and neighbors with the greeting, "Christ is born!" to which the other person responds "Glorify Him!" and wish each other "Merry Christmas," which brings joy and good cheer both to those giving greeting and those receiving it. Little children are just as capable of wishing someone "Merry Christmas" as adults are. In fact, when a little child wishes you "Merry Christmas," it is even more delightful both for you and for themselves.

If you want to try a more traditional way of caroling, you should get ready in advance. First, make an eight-pointed star. If you want, you can just cut it out of construction paper and then decorate it with bits of colored paper and glitter. Traditionally, the star carried around town was lit up from the inside by a lantern. These stars were also sometimes made out of wire or wooden dowels that were then decorated with colorful ribbons or colored paper.

The child who carries the star goes first and is the first to greet the people that live in each house and ask if they would like to listen to some Christmas caroling. Another child, holding a bell, can walk beside the child with the star so that people will hear the bell and know that carolers are coming. If you have several bells, several children can hold them and ring them. And someone else should carry a sack in case the people at whose houses you are caroling have treats for the children. You can make your own sack out of bright fabric and then decorate it a little with more fabric, colored paper, or tin foil, covering it with things like the sun and moon, stars, and snowflakes.

It is not a problem if you are not a good singer. You can sing along to simple Christmas carols with a group. And if your child is little, teach them even just a few lines and that will be a big accomplishment for them and a joy to listen to for everyone else.

GLOSSARY

Announcement (From a chapter title) - An announcement is a message, telling people about something new that has happened or is going to happen. You can point out to your child the connection with the word "Annunciation," when Mary received the "announcement" of the Good News, that she would give birth to the Savior.

Livestock - Livestock are domesticated animals like cows, sheep, bulls, and donkeys. Traditionally, a donkey and a bull are depicted near the Christ Child although they are not specifically mentioned either in the Gospel or in this book.

Swaddling clothes - Swaddling clothes are blankets used to wrap a newborn baby. Modern families also swaddle their infants. Point out the swaddling clothes to your child in the picture.

Glory to God in the highest and on earth peace, goodwill among men - This angelic hymn is easy for children to recognize because it is used in the Great Doxology at Church. There is not much to explain. This is "the language of the Angels." They are not singing to the shepherds but rather glorifying God. But if your children are curious and ask what the hymn means, you can tell them that "in the highest" means that God is over all things and that "goodwill" means that God loves all people and wants what is best for us.

Prophet - A prophet is a person who speaks on God's behalf. The prophets hear Him. Much of what they heard and told to others is contained in the Bible.

Magi - The Magi were wise men, Kings from the East. They were not the only ones to see the star but they were the only ones to understand what it meant and where it was leading them because of their great learning and piety.

www.ingramcontent.com/pod-product-compliance
Lightning Source LLC
Chambersburg PA
CBHW051350110526
44591CB00025B/2955